不醒

Lost in Reverie

A collection of Chinese prose poems with parallel English text

邓楠
Deng Nan

Translated by Christine Morris
Front cover design by Jonathan Rust

Copyright © 2017 Deng Nan
All rights reserved.
ISBN-13: 978-1545559130
ISBN-10: 1545559139

To everyone who has a tender heart

献给每一个温暖的人

目录/ Contents

南方的冬 / Southern Winter　　6/7
晚秋/ Late Autumn　　8/9
雾中城/ City in the Fog　　10/11
纵横/ Far and Wide　　12/13
三月清风/ Riding the March Breeze　　14/15
回声/ Echoes　　16/17
十字路口/ Crossroads　　18/19
短绽/ A Fleeting Bloom　　20/21
那一天/ One Day　　22/23
午夜巴黎/ Midnight in Paris　　24/25
海上花/ Flowers on the Water　　26/27
旧梦故园/ Old Dreams　　28/29
昨日之音/ A Voice from the Past　　30/31
湖之水/ To My Friend Hu　　32/33
空/ Emptiness　　34/35
致一位偶像/ To an Idol　　36/37
四季与你/ The Seasons and You　　38/39
两个夜晚/ Two Nights　　40/41
空镜/ Castles in the Air　　42/43
留白/ The Distance Between　　44/45
歌手/ The Singer　　46/47
与你暂借问/ Asking the Time　　48/49
我的一九九八/ Memories of 1998　　50/51
冉见不再见/ Goodbye Once More　　52/53
西湖/ West Lake　　54/55
往事/ Remembering　　56/57
离歌/ A Song of Farewell　　58/59
杨晨夜/ An Evening to Remember　　60/61
旧时现在/ Then and Now　　62/63
夜行/ Through the Night　　64/65
在水一方/ Across the Water　　66/67
聚散之间/ Meeting and Parting　　68/69
后记/ Postscript　　70/71

南方的冬

南方的冬，褪去夏日的轻浮，却不见严寒的逼仄，冷静与柔和交织，空气里吹来清香的风。白日里，骑着脚踏车在小巷间穿行，你向迎面来的人问好，面前的桃花就笑了。南方的冬天里，你不再想躲藏，任凭午后暖阳轻柔拥抱，久违的日头晒红了脸，你开口轻声说爱，却不再害羞。夜晚降临的时候，可以泛舟，两岸江火，像是天与地的交接，这时你若想要天上星，我就会跃入水中，为你捧出闪亮的露珠。

Southern Winter

In this southern winter, summer's frivolity has faded away, yet you do not feel hunched up against the bitter cold. A fragrant breeze wafts through the air, tranquility and sweetness intermingling. In the daytime, riding a bicycle through the narrow lanes, you say hello to passers-by and they in turn smile back. In this southern winter you no longer want to hide, but welcome the embrace of the warm afternoon sun. Your face glows from the sun it has not seen for so long and when you open your mouth to speak softly of love, you are no longer shy. When evening falls you can drift about in a boat, both sides of the river illuminated with a fiery glow, like the meeting point of heaven and earth. At this moment, if you wanted the stars in the sky, I would leap into the water and hold out to you sparkling dewdrops.

晚秋

晚秋的雾起又散,早春的雪落无踪,只因你的万种柔情从天而降。你是山水画中的一缕清风,你来过,无人知晓,你散去,余情难了。我该责怪载我与你相遇的列车,它不早不晚,送我的心于你的掌握。我没有怨恨你布下的雷池,你知道我会义无反顾,飞蛾扑火,你明知我如此善良。

Late Autumn

Late autumn fog descends than lifts,
Early spring snow falls then vanishes,
All because the air is filled with
A myriad of your tender feelings.
You are like a gentle breeze
In a landscape painting.
You come and go,
No-one notices.
The love you leave behind
Is hard to get over.
I should blame the train
For bringing us together
At just that moment in time,
Surrendering my heart to you.
I don't feel bitter
About the minefield you laid.
You know I will always sacrifice myself,
Like a moth darting into the flame.
You know I am so easily taken in.

雾中城

晚秋的北京下起大雾,就像盛夏的那阵暴雨,隆冬的那场白雪,轰轰烈烈。现在的我想和巴黎的你亲密小酌,再趁着夜色点一支烟,让铁塔的昏黄勾勒出你修长的轮廓。所以今夜我决定穿过浓雾,嘲笑的脸,冷漠的眼,慌张的人群,去寻找我的流光溢彩,繁花似锦。寻找到了你,就寻找到了家。

City in the Fog

A dense fog envelops late autumn in Beijing, like a midsummer storm, a fall of white snow in the depth of winter, grand and spectacular. I'd like to have an intimate glass of wine with you in Paris, then light a cigarette in the dim of the night, your tall thin figure silhouetted against the faint tower. So tonight I resolve to pass through the fog, the mocking faces, the cold and indifferent eyes, the rushing crowds and go in search of the lights and glamour ahead. Once I have found you, I have found home.

纵横

在异国大雨如注的街头,你愿为谁撑起手中伞。当他乡的霓虹闪烁,你又想燃亮谁的脸。我把每一次落脚当成驿站,而那未名的远方永远藏着新鲜的憧憬,此时彼刻唯有放逐才能活出自己的血肉精神。于是,当我把支离破碎的自己散落在万水千山,我又带着支离破碎的千山万水继续上路。

Far and Wide

In foreign climes, with the streets awash with rain, who would you like to shelter under your umbrella? In a place far from home, whose face would you like to see lit up by the flickering neon lights? Everywhere I rest my head is just a stage on my journey, a nameless distant place hiding fresh visions of the future. No matter whether then or now, only when I set myself free can I live true to my soul. So, when I scatter the fragments of myself across mountains and rivers, I continue on my journey carrying fragments of those countless places.

三月清风

三月,风和气暖,艳阳秀丽。乘醉人的春风,一起去江南看烟云般的花海,再飞去东京铁塔陪你做一个比日月更长久的梦,或策马在北方草原,看雄鹰高飞,天边落霞,和随落霞归家的羊群。虽然你在来路上迷失,而我失去了你的讯息。但我相信在阳光下我们总会相遇,终究我们会牵手旅行。

Riding the March Breeze

March brings the wind, warm air and beautiful bright sunshine. Riding on the intoxicating spring breeze, we'll travel together south of the Yangtze and look at the hazy seas of flowers. Then we'll fly to Tokyo Tower where we can dream a dream longer than life itself. Or we'll go horse riding on the northern grasslands, watch the eagles flying high in the sky, the red clouds sinking below the horizon and the sheep returning home in the evening glow of sunset. Although you lost your way here and I have no word from you, I'm certain that one day we'll find each other under the sunlight and at long last will journey together hand in hand.

回声

我有太多的欲望,让我不能去每一个爱慕的城市,寻找到同样爱慕文字的你。我们注定无法相逢,当湍急的欲望河流席卷,我们的前途未卜。但还好我们还能做一个好梦,就算这城市肮脏的看不到月光,砍掉所有的杏花树,我们买不起一杯酒。但我们写下了这些句子,说不清是幸福还是忧伤。

Echoes

I have too many desires making it impossible for me to go to every beloved city trying to find you who love words as I do. We are destined not to meet. When the fast-flowing river of our desire engulfs us our future is uncertain. But fortunately we can still dream a good dream, even if the city is too dirty to see the moonlight, even if all the apricot trees have been cut down, even if we cannot afford a glass of wine. However, we did write down these words. Who can say if they are happy or sad?

十字路口

陪伴这片熙来攘往不觉十年,日升月落,就如一夜一梦。想在两不相厌时离去,比起厮守,我们总是更擅长怀念。离去,趁我还把人山人海当做青春的温度,趁你还把我的不安以为真挚的徘徊,趁我还把梦的幻灭视为破晓的啼哭,趁你竟以为这无聊失眠是为你。也许我真的属于心中的海边,不必猜那一岸的云涌风起。

Crossroads

Keeping company with the hustle and bustle of life, without realising it, ten years have passed by. The sun rises, the moon falls, as if one dream in one night. I would like to leave before we two grow tired of each other. Compared to sharing a life together, we are always better at reminiscing. Leave while I still regard the hustle and bustle as the passion of youth, while you think my restlessness is merely pacing back and forth. Leave while I view the disillusionment of a dream as tears at daybreak, while you go so far as to think this boring insomnia is because of you. Perhaps in my heart I really belong by the sea; there is no need to guess that on the other shore lie trials and tribulations.

短绽

　　你紧捉春天的气息，游走在百花深处，便邂逅了一朵昙花。你把稍纵即逝的怒放藏在你温柔的心中，你知道唯有短暂才能免于蒙尘。在这荒谬尘世，你坐拥过繁华，又目击凋零，生活不过是聚散悲欢的又一次循环。你觉得你肯定会再回到这片百花深处，看昙花绽放瞬间，带着你被风霜摧毁的容颜。

A Fleeting Bloom

Catching hold of a breath of spring,
You wander through a sea of flowers
When you chance upon one
Which blossoms for just one day.
You hide the fleeting bloom in your tender heart,
Knowing that only that which is short-lived
Can escape from being tainted.
In this ridiculous world
You have collected fortune and plenty
And witnessed them wither away.
What is life but a cycle of parting and reuniting
Of joys and sorrows?
You are sure you will return to this sea of flowers
To look at your bloom's brief flash of glory,
Your looks destroyed by the hardships of life.

那一天

　　耀眼的一天胜过昏庸的一生，一生的不知所云倒不如用一天忘我的诠释。心底的轻颤，眼波的流转，藏着有情人的眷恋，形不露痕迹，神不着边际。千言万语，耳鬓厮磨只是俗世的庸人自扰。哪怕这一天的夕阳是生死的歧途，至少爱过，于浮世中，在尘嚣上，就这一天。

One Day

One bright day outshines one frivolous life; one day of showing your true self is better than a life without meaning. A fluttering heart, sidelong glances, these hide the longings of lovers, but there is no trace to be seen in your body or spirit. Those who talk incessantly, wrap themselves around each other are mere mortals making much ado about nothing. As the sun sets today, even if we take the wrong path between life and death, at least we have loved, in this fleeting world, just for one day.

午夜巴黎

午夜巴黎,午夜泄露了迷离,你无意间踏入时光,勾起了若有若无的过往。你觉得你该牵起一双手,趁巴黎还在,趁还有这午夜流光,一起淋一场大雨的浪漫,或在这行尸走肉间变得顽强。你觉得这世上太多混乱,倒不如在午夜去占领一片土地,最好就在巴黎,巴黎的午夜不带一丝慌张。

Midnight in Paris

Midnight in Paris
Reveals a blurriness;
Accidentally stepping back in time
You are plucked to a past
Which may or may not exist.
You think you should hold hands
While Paris is still here,
While the midnight moonlight is still here,
Get drenched in a romantic shower of rain
Or become stronger in this world
Full of the walking dead.
You think there is too much chaos in the world,
That it would be better
To seize a piece of land at midnight
Preferably in Paris.
Midnight in Paris
Holds not a trace of disquiet.

海上花

看繁花生于海上,上海如梦似真。曾驻足的驿站,总留些许情缘,才会日夜不舍。刚掠过你的天际,你留下的回忆已铺天盖地。我穿梭过细雨中的街道,恰有梧桐叶落,是你潜伏的线索。你此时的摩登,你那年的婉约,隔滔滔江水守望。一声吴侬软语轻叹,应伴人间轻浅小酌,不同红尘耿耿于怀。

Flowers on the Water

Looking at all the flowers blooming on the water, Shanghai is as real as a dream. Feelings of love still remain in the inn where I once stayed. Never will I part with them. Dipping over the horizon into your realm, the memories you left behind are overwhelming. I wander up and down the streets in the light rain, the falling leaves of the plane trees your hidden clues. The present modern you and the past elegant you keep watch separated by the flowing river. A soft sigh in the Wu dialect: we should have a drink to life and not take the world's troubles to heart.

旧梦故园

故园藏着旧梦，于一花一树间，看得到时光的身影，它奔跑在无尽长路，偶尔回首惆怅。故园住着昔日的你，那个昔日黄昏中的你，那些你们并肩依偎的昔日黄昏。日落前，你看到红色的天，害羞的脸。落日后，你们看不见彼此，却紧捉住那双手。只是这岁月太长，我只好把旧梦留给了故园。

Old Dreams

Old dreams
Are hiding in my hometown.
You can see Time's silhouette
In every tree and flower
It rushes along the endless road ahead,
Occasionally looking back in melancholy.
In my hometown lived the past me,
That past me in the twilight,
Those twilight evenings
When we nestled up against each other.
Before sunset I see a red sky, a shy face.
After sunset, no longer able to see each other
Yet tightly we keep hold of each other's hands.
However life is too long
I have to leave my dreams to my hometown.

昨日之音

　　白日飞扬的柳絮也已睡去,空荡荡的街上,洒水车独自排遣寂寞。和昔日好友短暂重逢,粗茶淡饭间,昨日从远处回首,它正与今夜清凉的晚风问候。这寂静小路上,步履踏着月影,空气里渗透着尘土气息,朴素的情侣低声轻语。喧嚣散尽,坚持依旧,路就这样沉默地走。夜便无端多了美好。

A Voice from the Past

The willow catkins, floating around all day, have finally settled down. On the deserted street a solitary sprinkler truck shakes off its loneliness. Meeting up with an old friend over a simple meal, it seems the distant past has come back to greet tonight's breeze. Walking along this quiet street, stepping on the moon's shadow, the air thick with the smell of dust, a pair of simple lovers quietly chatter. The noise and clamour have died down and I quietly walk along, still following the same path as before. For no real reason, tonight has just become more beautiful.

湖之水

如果不是等候花开,你不会捱过寒冬的冷漠,迎面暖风正吹开了深锁的明媚。你走在寻常的路上,这两旁终于变得不同寻常,你相信是因为春天和你天真的约会。只是这城市还缺了一池湖水,你便可以抚一曲琴,布一局棋,捧一本书,就爱上了那画中人。你填满沧海,建起孤岛,你自封为王,却把钥匙送给了爱情。

To My Friend Hu

If it wasn't for the promise of the flowers coming into bloom, you could never get through the cold indifference of winter. Now the warm wind is blowing open the radiance which has been locked away for so long. You walk along your ordinary path when, after a while, both sides become extraordinary and you believe this is because of your innocent date with spring. All this city needs is a lake and then you could play the zither, set up a chessboard, read a book, fall in love with the characters in the picture. You fill up the deep blue sea, build a desert island, proclaim yourself king, yet surrender the key to love.

空

　　秋天真的到了，你真的不会回到这座城市了。昨日他离去，今天你不见，我饮下了无常的血，血腥苦涩，当风吹冷了夜。当天他的再见成了永别，当天你的转身又是曲终。当天就像是漫长数年，波涛汹涌。时间是孩子眼中的一场虚无，而我是一个孩子，想念他在天堂，想念你在天边。

Emptiness

Autumn has really arrived. You are really not returning to this city. Yesterday he left, today I can no longer see you. Life dealt me an unexpected blow, bloody and bitter, the wind blowing cold in the night. That day his goodbye turned into a final farewell, that day your turning away was also the end of the song. That day seemed to last forever, turmoil raging all around. Time holds no meaning to a child, so I am a child, missing him in heaven, missing you to the ends of the earth.

致一位偶像

又一颗星坠落,黑暗奔走狂欢。想用这首歌纪念你。纪念用五元钱去看一次《保镖》的镭射厅,纪念一个喜欢你却更喜欢我的女孩。我还想纪念你演绎的电影,那些爱别离求不得,我们将用一生去学习。还有你哼唱的旋律,像夜归路上划亮的一根火柴,总有些温度,有些光芒,当我们与孤独分庭抗礼。

To an Idol

Another star falls and darkness rushes in celebrating noisily. I would like to remember you with this song; to remember paying five dollars to go and see "The Bodyguard" on video in the local hall; to remember a girl who liked you but who liked me even more. I would also like to pay tribute to your performance in the film. Saying farewell to those you love, not finding what you are searching for, we will all experience this sometime in our lives. Then there is you humming a melody, like lighting a match on the way home at night, there is always some warmth and radiance when we make a stand against loneliness.

四季与你

春花、夏夜、秋蝉、冬雪，我介意的不是风景不够极致，而是你一再缺席。冬寒、秋霜、夏雨、春风，我担心的不是天气阴晴不定，而是和你相遇的可能。寒冬压境、春风化雨、夏花灿烂、一叶知秋，坐看四季变换，静候你的出现。

The Seasons and You

Spring flowers, summer nights, autumn cicadas, winter snow; what I care about is not that the scenery is less than sublime, but that you are forever absent. Cold winters, autumn frosts, summer rains, spring winds; what I worry about is not if the weather is cloudy or clear but whether or not I will see you. Winter draws near, spring breezes turn to rain, summer flowers burst into bloom, the first leaves begin to fall. I sit watching the seasons change, waiting for you to appear.

两个夜晚

　　日出之前,乘计程车离开,清醒的告别总是艰难。你幻想终点可以倒流回起点,如同起身一刻你竟希望自己能变幻成这寻常生活中的一介小民,真挚平淡地于此地生、老、病、死。我们眷恋的不是一段路途,却是一种情怀,当我们的纯净消失在窒息的办公桌前,拥挤的人潮中,还有那注惨白的灯光下。我们缅怀的不是一种情怀而是一次放逐。当你脱掉华服,露出柔软,我用唇轻抚你温热的身体,我还听得见心跳的起伏。于是,我选择在日出之前,乘计程车离开,清醒的告别总是艰难,所以昨夜酒醉不眠。

Two Nights

You leave in a taxi before the sun rises; a sober farewell is always difficult. You picture being able to go back to the beginning and starting over again. It's as if the moment you set out you actually wish you could become a mere nobody in an ordinary life; simply be born, grow old, fall ill and die. When our freshness disappears behind our suffocating desks, amongst the hordes of people and under the harsh bright lights, what we miss most is not one particular journey but the sensations it brings. What we will remember are not the sensations but the feeling of being set free. When you took off your fine clothes baring your softness, I caressed your warm body with my lips, listening to the rhythm of your heartbeat. So, I chose to leave in a taxi before sunrise. A sober farewell is always difficult, so last night I lay in a state of drunken sleeplessness.

空镜

灰暗的冰雨袭来,在你以为春天尽在掌握。若有所思地穿行在潮湿的迷宫中,用脚步胡乱勾画关于你的涂鸦。你一定有尘嚣之上孩子纯真的笑脸,能融化早春的寒意。像雨夜笼罩下那亲切的一盏光,温暖因此坚强不灭。我想我该继续走在路上,如果这时有风,就会与你在花开的地方狭路相逢。

Castles in the Air

Just when you think spring is truly in your grasp, dark ice cold rain hits. Lost in thought, I cross the wet labyrinth of the city and with meandering steps sketch a picture of you in my mind. You must have the smiling face of an innocent child to be able to melt away the early spring chill. It is as if your comforting glow shines through the rainy night, the warmth intense and constant. I would like to continue along this road. If now the wind were to spring up, then we are destined to meet in a place full of blossoming flowers.

留白

　　白色月台上，或许是春暖花开前的最后一场雪，把心留给身后的家，列车终点将停靠在滚滚红尘。我想，那终究是无法挣脱的归宿。酒醉的人们在街头游荡，步履混乱，却快乐地唱着那些悲伤的歌。你们呼出白色水雾，像是把心融化给了你藏匿旧情的这片方寸。你回来过，又看到了失去的你，这旅途就并非徒有虚名。

The Distance Between

You stand on the white platform, perhaps the last fall of snow before spring comes and the flowers bloom, and leave your heart behind with your home. The train will be heading back to the hustle and bustle of the world. I think, in the end, there is no way of breaking free from your destination. Some drunken people are wandering along the street, staggering from side to side but happily singing those sad songs. You breathe out a white vapour, as if you are giving your melting heart to this place which hides your memories from bygone days. You have come back, found again the person you once were. This has been more than just a journey.

歌手

去年今夕，雨落满天，和她不期而遇。多年前，她曾站在远方，她站在远方的那晚，我看远方飞沙走石，大雨纷纷。多年后，她忍心放下执着，辗转尘世情怀，那光怪陆离的江湖只是一段传说。今晚京城春雨飘洒，我行走雨中，身不由己，冷暖自知。这雨水若幻化成酒，能否痛饮，无论为谁。

The Singer

On this night last year, the sky filled with rain, I happened to meet her. Years earlier she had stood in a faraway place and on that evening in that faraway place I had seen dust and stones flying and rain lashing down. Years later she gave up on her obsession, realising that kaleidoscopic world of entertainment was just an illusion. Tonight, as Beijing's spring rain swirls in the air, I have no choice but to walk through it, only I knowing how things are for me. If this rain were to turn into wine, could I drink it down no matter for whom?

与你暂借问

你也有过这样鲁莽的经历?把手表藏进衣袖,借问时间;在熟悉的路旁,故作迷路。不知是想和美好多共存一秒,还只是想试探自己的心有没有动的可能。总之,我从没有说出口,"其实,我知道怎么走,问你,只是想和你说话"。因为我知道这话说了,就是一部电影。不说呢,才是生活。

Asking the Time

Have you ever done something impulsive like this? I hide my watch under my sleeve and ask for the time, pretending to be lost on this road I know so well. I don't know whether I do this just so I can stand side by side with beauty for a second longer or if it's simply to see if my heart can still be set fluttering. Anyway, I didn't come out with the words, "Actually, I know the way and I'm only asking you because I want to talk to you." I know that's what they would say in a film but in real life I say nothing.

我的一九九八

1998年,说来竟如此遥远。你抽的烟,被西北来的风吹散,吹过你绯红的笑脸,堆积在我成长的行囊中。而你的歌声总躲藏在破旧的收音机里,那台收音机固执地和我决裂在中原的小城。他们说,你的心智失散,而我觉得,是这个世界荒唐。今天,我也是这城市的夜归人,等待夜归的梦中人。

Memories of 1998

When you say 1998, it already seems so long ago. Your cigarette smoke is blown away by the north-west wind, blows across your flushed cheeks, accumulates in my life's baggage. Your song is always hiding in that battered old radio, that radio which finally parted company from me in a small town in central China. They say you lost your mind but rather I think it is this world which is absurd. Today I am also a wanderer in this city returning home late at night, waiting for a wanderer to return into my dreams.

再见不再见

如果你写一本书是为了寻找人海中的我,那我杯中的咖啡就溶化了十年等待的流光。重逢是为了再次告别,正如上次告别是为了见到你经年后的模样。当我弹起吉他跳起轻快的华尔兹,你像窗前的小猫安详凝望。你的航班就要起飞,而我的心将在日暮前陪你翱翔。

Goodbye Once More

If you are writing a book to try and find me in this world full of people, then my cup of coffee will make the past ten years of waiting disappear. Being reunited is to say goodbye once again, just as saying goodbye last time was to see you again years later. When I start playing the guitar, start dancing a frolicsome waltz, you gaze contentedly like a cat at the window. Your flight is about to depart, but my heart will soar with you before sunset.

西湖

午后,泛舟于粼粼波光的水面,听船夫三言两语,讲那些寄托于这片风景的童话。我被阳光灌醉,昏昏欲睡,他的话就讲给了水中的鱼儿听。晒过暖阳,坐在青年旅舍,慵懒弥漫心头,和可爱的江南女孩闲聊,只言片语间,岁月被日头拉扯,黄昏就慢慢降临。与青春交手,最终同时光握手言和,爱情就成了身外之物。

West Lake

Drifting in a boat one afternoon

On the crystal clear sunlit waves,

Listening to the boatman

Laconically telling fairy tales about the places,

I feel intoxicated by the sunlight, drowsy,

Only the fish in the water are listening to his words.

After basking in the warm sun

Feeling languid

I sit in the youth hostel,

Exchange a few words with a sweet southern girl.

Shadows stretch out in the sun,

Dusk slowly falls.

Wrestling with youth,

I finally call a truce with Time,

Love has become disconnected.

往事

回忆是天堂投递的情书,有故事的人才懂用心朗读。青春赴汤蹈火,万劫不复,故事却历久弥新,在情怀间传唱。我只要这个夜晚,让你想起不曾遗忘的留恋,你懂了,这兵荒马乱才找到了动人的始终。雨后北京微凉,异国的初夏轻柔,你折起这封情书,你的笑,像星辉洒满前路。

Remembering

Memories are love letters delivered by heaven, people with a story to tell know to read them from the heart. Gone forever is youth when you went through fire and water, yet as time passes memories become clearer, passed on from soul to soul. This evening all I want is to let you recall those never to be forgotten nostalgic feelings. Only when you understand them can you find the real story for the turmoil and chaos of this world. After the rain Beijing is cool, the exotic early summer is gentle. You fold away this love letter, your smile like a star shining upon the road ahead.

离歌

　　车水马龙中，渐渐松开握住的手，转身紧抱住失落。这城池中的断壁残垣，还要独自披星戴月地走过。你的背包藏着一幅爱情地图，上面标注着你屡败屡战的过往。你一路风雨迢迢，探访世上所有单纯的美好，此时你用夜曲一首相送曼谷的温柔。你徒劳无功地追随远去的背影，你能听见心碎，融化在夜晚的车水马龙。

A Song of Farewell

Amidst the flurry of the traffic
Slowly let go hands, turn away,
Embrace your loss.
Through this derelict city
You wander alone hours on end.
Hidden in your baggage a map of love
Marks all your failures and constant struggles.
Coming through life's hardships
You seek out the simple beauties of the world.
Here and now
Dedicate a song to the warmth of Bangkok.
In vain you follow the receding figure.
You hear the sound of your heart breaking
Melt into the clamour of the night.

杨晨夜

这些日子总觉得天空太灰,街道太脏,想掩面逃亡,到任何一个不叫做北京的地方。走出十点钟的那扇门,街灯下的夜晚依然不够清澈,但人却像喝了一场好酒,飘忽地穿行在几乎厌倦的生活中,如同一个被赋予了爱的天使。我想今夜将是好梦,和你醉在倾城的月光里。

An Evening to Remember

These days I always feel the sky is too grey, the streets too dirty. I want to cover my face with my hands and flee to any city other than Beijing. Coming out of the theatre door at ten o'clock, it is still not clear enough under the streetlights, yet it is as if we are all light-headed from a bout of merry drinking. Like an angel with the gift of love, I float through this life I was once so weary of. I think tonight I will dream sweet dreams, to be drunk with you in this beautiful moonlight.

旧时现在

在春天遇到冬天里爱过的人,像在烈日追赶下怀念北国的白雪皑皑,心动被悄然错失。你靠在玻璃窗上,窗内觥筹交错的热烈,窗外惶惶的匆忙告别,人生的一场场悲喜交加。而你和映在玻璃窗上的你,一个如天使般柔情,一个却如此陌生遥远。听说时间是冰冷杀手,我却希望回忆永垂不朽。

Then and Now

In Spring,
Chancing upon one you loved in winter,
Is like yearning for the pure white snow of the North
While being chased by the hot sun.
No longer is your heart set pounding.
You lean against the window;
Inside, all is feasting and making merry,
Outside, all is hasty goodbyes,
Life's joys and sorrows side by side.
You and your reflection in the window,
One tender as an angel,
The other distant as a stranger.
They say that time is a cold killer
But I hope that memories never die.

夜行

拨开夜晚的寂静,驾车穿行在孤独的乡间,当黑暗只留下一盏月光,我才敢紧握你的手,于忽明忽暗的路上。这段路若多些漫长,我就会带你飞向夺目的光明。静谧夏夜,唯见流星几颗划过,共饮的一杯茶浸润唇角,胜过海市蜃楼堆砌的繁华。无声无言中我读懂了藏在你眉眼中的秘密,你看这世界,已是鸟语花香。

Through the Night

Pushing through the tranquility of the night, we drive through the lonely countryside. In the darkness, only when there is just the moonlight flickering on the road, do I dare to grasp your hand. If this stretch of road was a little longer I could fly you to the dazzling brightness. On this still summer night all you can see are a few meteors streaking across the sky. We sip our shared cup of tea, better than any fancy mirage. Needing no words I understand the secrets hidden in your eyes. Look at this world; it has become a Garden of Eden.

在水一方

　　据说阳光总爱不期而至,又不告而别。和你贪婪地晒着可遇不可求的温暖,我们是这世界上难得的人。眯着眼睛,面向天空,内心柔软。相遇,像入夜后凌空绽放的烟火,在不寻常的时刻昙花一现。小憩在水中央的鸬鹚,周折于南北,只凭着对幸福的嗅觉。而我,来回游走,匆忙落跑,与不安擦肩,和美好相见恨晚。

Across the Water

They say that the sun likes to arrive unexpectedly and leave without saying goodbye. Basking in this unlooked-for sunshine, we two are special people in this world. Squinting up at the sky, we feel warm and mellow inside. Our encounter is like the dazzle of fireworks high in the night sky, an extraordinary fleeting moment. A heron takes rest in the middle of the water; flying between north and south, it relies only on its senses to find happiness. As for me, wandering back and forth, hurriedly making getaways, crossing paths with restlessness, how I wish we could have met earlier.

聚散之间

　　春夏秋冬是你眼中跌宕的宇宙，可你不过是这宇宙的偶然回眸。雪夜围炉，天地苍白，而君心火红，你在等待一双眼，盼浮现在旧岁消失前。终于，离人披着风霜， 踏着白雪，掀开牵挂，带着异乡的温度，和你并肩坐在火热的炕床上。把酒言欢，诉重逢，却不提愁肠。顿时，刀光剑影的世间苍茫终抵不过这一寸韶光。

Meeting and Parting

In your eyes, the passing of time is the ebb and flow of the Universe but to the Universe you are merely an accidental backwards glance. A snowy night around the fire, the entire world white, your heart is full of anticipation. You are waiting for a pair of eyes, hoping they will appear before the old year disappears. At last, with the hardships of life draped over his shoulders, treading on the white snow, the wanderer opens the door to cares and worries, bringing temperatures from foreign lands. Sitting side by side on the hot *kang we raise a glass and talk cheerfully, speak about reunions, but not about our worries. Suddenly, these precious moments are worth all the fierce struggles we have endured.

*kang - *a brick platform built across one end of a room in a house in northern China, warmed by a fire beneath and used for sleeping*

后记

写这段话时,中国北方又要进入漫长严寒。对于当下的你们,请珍重挺过这一冬。而如果你是数十数百年后的人类,我想说,你看,这时代变了,这爱恨悲欢,这一段欲说还休是如此雷同。

Postscript

As I write these words, northern China is starting its long cold winter. To those of you reading this now, take good care as you endure the bitter months ahead. If you are reading this hundreds of years in the future, I'd like to say: you see, time has moved on but love and hate, joy and sorrow, all these remain the same.

About the Author

Deng Nan was born in Inner Mongolia, China and studied English Language and Literature at university. He originally started writing short pieces for the Chinese micro-blogging site Sina Weibo inspired both by his travels around the world and China and memories of his life in the past.

About the Translator

Christine Morris studied Modern Chinese Studies at Leeds University, UK and went on to live and work in China for many years where she developed her love of Chinese literature and translating.

Contact the writer at: lostinreverie@fastmail.com

Printed in Great Britain
by Amazon